STRAWBERRY AND THE BIG APPLE

STRAWBERRY AND THE BIG APPLE

Grace Jones in Stockport, 1980

DAVE HASLAM

First published in the UK in 2024 by Cōnfingō Publishing

249 Burton Road, Didsbury, Manchester, M20 2WA
www.confingopublishing.uk

Cover design by Zoë McLean
Typesetting by John Oakey

Printed by TJ Books Limited

A CIP catalogue record for this book is available from the British Library

ISBN 978-1-7393745-4-9

2 4 6 8 10 9 7 5 3 1

If you were in New York, Studio 54 was the place to be on New Year's Eve at the end of 1977, the first New Year's Eve in what turned out to be Studio 54's spectacular but short history. Partygoers at the venue that evening included the American fashion designer Halston, artist Andy Warhol, and Nicaraguan actress Bianca Jagger. There's a photograph purporting to be from that evening suggesting Michael Jackson was there, dressed for the occasion in a rather downbeat brown and beige tank top, and a light brown jacket, and in the company of Liza Minnelli.

In her autobiography *I'll Never Write My Memoirs* – a cheeky title deriving from a phrase in her song 'Art Groupie' – Grace Jones reckons she met Marianne Faithfull that New Year's Eve, even though Marianne Faithfull claims she never went to Studio

54. 'She was definitely there, unless I'm making it up,' writes Grace. 'Maybe it was the only time she went. I remember it well, because that was the moment [Marianne] introduced me to Cocoa Puffs; marijuana cigarettes laced with cocaine.'[1]

Grace Jones was a key part of the entertainment. Given that at Studio 54 you might witness nudity, roller-skating, Truman Capote on the dancefloor, a marching band of Rockettes, or Dolly Parton stroking a horse – possibly, but not necessarily, all on the same night – there could be no holding back when it came to New Year's Eve. Surrounded by dancers, Grace Jones took to the stage at around three o'clock in the morning, singing three songs to a backing tape, wearing a clingy, revealing, shiny gold unitard over a shimmering bodysuit, with added sparkle and feathers, and silver knee-high boots.

It was a Norma Kamali-designed costume. Kamali was a celebrated designer whose work had been worn by Farrah Fawcett, one of the stars of the TV series *Charlie's Angels*. A photograph taken at Fawcett's estate in Los Angeles – where she was living with her partner Lee Majors – featuring the actress wearing a red, one-piece Kamali-designed swimsuit became

[1] Grace Jones, *I'll Never Write My Memoirs* (Simon & Schuster, 2015), 164.

the biggest-selling poster in history. The poster has its own Wikipedia entry.

No one could be surprised that Farrah Fawcett was popular. She glistened with all the traditional attributes of a pin-up; she was white, with luxuriant blonde hair, an exemplary, friendly smile, a weekly audience on TV, and wholesomeness galore. Grace Jones, on the other hand, was dark black, Jamaican, a challenge, unreadable, with an ambiguity about her look – 'I am very feminine, but I am also extremely masculine. I've got these two things going on,' she later declared.[2] The way she conquered prevailing perceptions of what constitutes beauty is among the many achievements in her life.

At Studio 54 that New Year's Eve, Grace Jones's performance was as much about theatre and fashion as it was about music. She maintains that Kabuki stillness onstage suited her better than dancing ('I wasn't so great a dancer'), although she'd use the whole stage to crawl all over the place, hissing, and barking like an animal on the prowl. Then she started wielding a whip, and her reputation soared.

With a love of acting, and experience as a model, Grace Jones knew how to play a role. The

---

[2] Ibid., 114.

onstage persona carried through to the parts she was to play in films in the 1980s including *Conan the Destroyer* (1984) and the Bond movie *A View to a Kill* (1985). Nick Stewart, a former A&R man at Island Records who worked closely with Grace Jones in 1979 and 1980 during and after the release of the *Warm Leatherette* album, has a take on the myths surrounding her. 'What you have to remember about Grace, Dave, is that she's a preacher's daughter from Jamaica and while people were quite scared of her – a legacy of some of the stuff she got up to in nightclubs and later that role in the Bond movie – she was, and is, a really sweet person. I don't want to destroy a myth here, but she's good company, gentle in some ways.'

I'm talking to Nick via Zoom. He's taking two dogs for a walk; I'm at my desk, clutching magazines carrying interviews with Grace Jones, and a copy of her autobiography. I read out a quote from her: 'I'm two people. Otherwise I'd be insane.'

'The performer and the private person. I think that's a good call,' he agrees.

During 1977, Grace Jones had released her debut album *Portfolio*, on a label called Beam Junction (distributed by Island Records) who put her in Sigma Sound Studios in Philadelphia with disco record producer Tom Moulton. *Portfolio* comprised mostly covers; songs from Broadway musicals including 'Tomorrow' from Annie, and 'Send in the Clowns' by Stephen Sondheim, alongside a seven-minute reinterpretation of Edith Piaf's 'La Vie en rose', and a track that became a big dancefloor hit, 'I Need a Man'.

Grace had originally released 'I Need a Man' in France years earlier but the single had made little impact either side of the Atlantic. The song was given a rework by Tom Moulton, who'd worked on Gloria Gaynor releases. His versions of 'I Need a Man' were aimed directly at the dancefloor; extended landscapes of sound very identifiable as disco, lush, pulsating.

'I Need a Man' still didn't make a widespread impact but achieved sizeable pockets of popularity, including, most significantly, the gay disco crowd. In an interview with Chris Salewicz in *The Face* magazine in 1980, Grace Jones discusses the song's status as a 'a gay national anthem', pointing out the key role of gay clubs – most often specifically black gay clubs – at the vanguard of disco.[3]

Later, when Grace was working with Jean-Paul Goude there was always a dramatic aesthetic in the way she was being represented visually – but this was the case earlier in her career too. The sleeve of the

---

[3] *The Face*, October 1980.

Portfolio album was designed by Richard Bernstein whose work gave a distinctive look to the front covers of Andy Warhol's *Interview* magazine. The album cover is a close-up of Grace's head, her fierce look tempered by patches of purple, and turquoise eye shadow. It was an airbrushed, fantasy version of reality.

+

After *Portfolio*, Grace Jones released two more disco albums with Tom Moulton – *Fame* (1978) and *Muse* (1979). But at the start of the 1970s, she would have doubted anyone who told her that by the end of the decade she'd have had three albums to her name. Her mother, a lyric soprano, had an incredible, pure voice, but Grace didn't feel blessed: 'I never really thought I could sing at all, because my voice was so deep and manly.'[4]

Grace grew up the third in a family of six children in a middle-class household in Jamaica, and was known in her childhood as Beverly or Bev. Music was a part of her upbringing but exclusively in the context of religion and church going. She had a close ally: her gay brother Chris. His sexuality triggered conflicts at

---

[4] Jones, *Memoirs*, 55.

home. 'My dad was very uncomfortable at the time with Chris being gay. It was one of the worst things for a pastor to cope with in quiet, very repressed suburbia.'[5]

Grace had no shortage of advice from her parents, including a suggestion that she should be a lawyer or teacher. Her mother had married a preacher; that was also a suggestion for Grace, but the chances of Grace following this advice were slim. A natural-born contrarian, she later wrote that she was always 'going upstream when everyone else is going downstream'.[6]

The Jones family moved to Syracuse in upstate New York in search of a better life in the United States. Her parents went first, leaving Chris and Grace in the care of Grace's maternal grandmother and her step-grandfather, a Pentecostal bishop they called Mas P. 'A sadist,' she says.

Once in Syracuse, she began calling herself by her middle name, Grace. At college, where she was studying with a view to becoming a language teacher or interpreter, she bonded with a drama teacher called Tom Figenshu, indulging in long conversations about art and Jack Kerouac and John Cassavetes. He

---

[5] Ibid., 47.
[6] Ibid., 58.

invited her to take part in a theatre show during a
school summer break. Grace didn't hesitate. 'Taking
to a stage seemed very natural because the church is
like a show, it's an act; you're onstage, surrounded by
other people who want to be taken somewhere, who
want to believe in something.'[7]

In the late 1960s, Grace Jones was moving
beyond her teenage years, and living in Philadelphia.
Surfing the sea of possibilities the sixties were offering
her, Grace stayed in a hippie commune, became a go-
go dancer, took risks, took acid, spent a summer living
as a nudist, and rode with the Hell's Angels.

These wanderings were all good and life-en-
hancing, but the need to earn money couldn't be ig-
nored. Tom suggested that she could do some modelling while her acting progressed, so she sought out
Tony Barboza, an African American photographer
working in New York. Their first session included
headshots and nudes (to Grace, there was nothing
lewd about posing nude). Her first modelling job
came through Tony; it was for *Essence* magazine in
1970. She was photographed with the psychedelic soul
group the Chambers Brothers, wearing tight, studded
brown leather, looking very badass.

---

[7] Ibid., 56.

Grace Jones was pursuing an acting career, but modelling was bringing in some cash. In 1973, she appeared on the front cover of a Billy Paul album – the re-release of *Ebony Woman*. Her profile was non-existent, though; she's not identified on the cover. And there's no photographer credit.

In her memoirs, she admits that while endorsing the idea of an 'ebony woman' she didn't think of herself as black, at least not in an African American way. She had an Afro, but she didn't have a black American accent. She says she felt one remove from the black community in New York. She was Jamaican: 'I just didn't sound hip and Harlem enough when I opened my mouth'.

Her search for film roles was undermined by her agency's assertion, 'Your face doesn't fit.' Being told your face doesn't fit could elicit all kinds of responses. Grace Jones had the strength to turn a negative into a positive. This is another of her achievements; she's created her own space, her desire and ability to resist categorisation is striking.

Moving on, she signed up to modelling agent Wilhelmina Cooper who had an eye for unusual looks, although when Grace unilaterally decided to get rid of her hair, Cooper was outraged and the new look nearly lost Grace her agency's support. In her memoirs she explains that shaving her head was a conscious challenge – 'I was always wanting to test people, provoke them into a reaction'.[8]

In 1973, Grace Jones was 25 and living in the Big Apple with her brother Chris. Her brother was working as a DJ. Between them, they knew most of what club culture had to offer; inside knowledge was key in an era when the best dance venues were often out of sight, down unlit streets. These were the first days of disco in New York. Grace's brother Chris was working at a club called Hippopotamus on East 62nd Street.

Wilhelmina Cooper eventually concluded Grace was too out there to secure much modelling work in the States; the catwalk and catalogue bookers preferred a blander look. She suggested going to Europe, telling Grace 'they will understand you in a way they won't here'.

Taking an opportunity to relocate to a new city, especially one with the potential of Paris, can provide room for adventure, and perhaps suggest a new a path. Grace grew fond of Paris: 'I would find a home in Paris, and most of my formative years were spent there'.[9]

---

[8] Ibid., 81.
[9] Ibid., 99.

She was signed to a Paris agency called Euro Planning, later known as Prestige. Remarkably, the first three models on their books were Jerry Hall, Grace Jones, and Jessica Lange. Grace and Jerry Hall spent countless nights out in Paris painting the town rouge. Grace's favourite night out was at Club Sept, run by Fabrice Emaer on rue Sainte-Anne featuring DJ Guy Cuevas. Grace was often the last to arrive and the last to leave. 'I know that I was the wildest party animal ever. I pushed myself to the limit and started from there.'[10]

One of the young women working at Euro Planning had a boyfriend who was hoping to make it in the music business. He persuaded Grace to take part in a studio session. She sang 'Dirty Ol' Man' by the Three Degrees, generating some useful feedback: take singing lessons. But the experience was enough for Grace to persuade herself to focus on music.

Within four years, she had made plenty of headway: a single big on the best dancefloors, a debut album, and a burgeoning reputation as a performer. Fabrice Emaer opened a new club in March 1978, Le Palace, very much inspired by Studio 54, with Guy Cuevas again on DJ duties. The opening night featured

---

[10] Ibid., 175.

Grace Jones. Thousands of people crammed into the venue: 'It was quite an occasion,' Grace recalled later. 'The coke laid on was tinted pink.'[11]

+

Stockport is a town seven miles south of Manchester, featuring what's said to be the largest brick-built structure in northern Europe, the railway viaduct. In November 1980, Grace Jones paid a visit to the town, specifically to Strawberry Studios, pursuing an idea of recording songs with A Certain Ratio, who were then signed to Factory Records. The visit of a spectacularly glamorous jet-setting singer to Stockport sounds wonderfully improbable. Whatever its qualities and claims to fame, Stockport is unlikely to have ever been spoken about in the same breath as New York, or Paris.

Towns close to Manchester grew and prospered in the nineteenth century through the manufacture of cotton and various textile trades. Stockport was a mill town known for the production of silk, and for hat-making. Industrial might came at a price, however, in the form of ceaseless exploitation of the workforce and poor living conditions. Friedrich Engels described

---

[11] Ibid., 166.

Stockport as one of the 'duskiest, smokiest holes' in the area. Looking from the train, he said, the view of the town is 'repellent'.[12]

In the 1930s, and particularly after the Second World War, there was a falling away of the textile and associated trades. However, the problems of competition from overseas and underinvestment at home were masked in the early 1960s during an era of full employment, with teenagers and the young enjoying a decent disposable income, but the decade staggered to an end with optimism fading. By the end of the 1970s, concern about rising unemployment in Stockport led to questions to the Secretary of State for Employment in the House of Commons. Redundancy notices in Stockport were running at over four hundred a month.

In the summer of 1978, a few months after Grace Jones lit up Le Palace, former Sex Pistols singer John Lydon – who'd been fundamental to the punk explosion of 1976 – was bringing together a new group, Public Image Ltd. Once defined and pinned down, any emergent genre or art movement has the potential to become predictable. Derivative rather than creative. But, to escape the albatross of cultural conservatism,

---

[12] Friedrich Engels, *The Condition of the Working-Class in England in 1844* (Cosimo Classics, 2009), 43.

Lydon and PiL delivered a new injection of the original punk ethos of way-out inventiveness.

This reassertion of radicalism wasn't limited to the former Sex Pistol. By the time of PiL's second album, *Metal Box*, there was a plethora of glorious spiky, dubby, weirdo bands like the Slits, the Pop Group, Cabaret Voltaire, Joy Division, A Certain Ratio, the Fall. These acts all had some connection to the energy of punk but in addition displayed a wide palate of influences – including Kraftwerk, Brian Eno, Can, dub reggae, Funkadelic, Don Cherry. The 'post-punk' label wasn't in use at the time, but in retrospect has been tied to these bands and (dozens) more. In addition, it's also often avowed that post-punk music was, in part, a product of, and a soundtrack to, the post-industrial landscape of decayed industry, and semi-derelict buildings.

In the summer of 1978, A Certain Ratio consisted of just two young men, Pete Terrell and Simon Topping, but by the end of September 1978, Jez Kerr and Martin Moscrop were added. Their first gig as a four-piece was at Band on the Wall, with the Passage. Roughly seventy-five people attended, and their fee was £20.

The venues ACR were playing – dank basements, dilapidated function rooms – also included

STRAWBERRY AND THE BIG APPLE

the Factory, in Hulme. Factory presented live music at a venue called the Russell Club; the Russell was also known as the PSV, having been a club created for drivers and other public service vehicle workers. One of Factory's co-founders, Tony Wilson, had a high-profile presenting job on Granada TV. Among his shows was *So It Goes* (1976/7) which featured live music. Granada, based in the North-West, had a strong identity that reached the attention of the nation with programmes including *Coronation Street* and *World in Action.*

Joy Division manager Rob Gretton witnessed one early ACR show at Band on the Wall and recommended them to Tony Wilson. At the time, Wilson, in addition to the Factory nights, and a fledgling music management company, was working towards developing a Factory record label. There were plans afoot to include Joy Division on the new label's first vinyl release, a compilation showcasing several bands.[13]

Despite – or more probably, because of – ACR's unpolished and leftfield approach, Tony Wilson became their manager, and financed some studio time for a debut single at Cargo recording studios in Rochdale. 'All Night Party' became the second vinyl offering from Factory. In this period, ACR and Joy Di-

---

[13] This would eventually be released in January 1979.

vision played at Eric's, Liverpool; the fee was £66 for
both bands to share and a tenner each for expenses.[14]

'All Night Party' was hardly the soundtrack to
an all-night party anyone would wish to attend. The
world of Studio 54 was a craving after fantasy, and – in
the words of Grace Jones – a 'show-business illusion'.
ACR's debut single, on the other hand, was sombre,
angsty, conjuring bad drugs in Hulme, and the harsh
reality of the empty city. ACR had short-back-and-
sides and baggy 'demob' trousers; they dressed as if
Manchester was still in the 1940s, and the band were
living in a world of rationing, austerity, and not much
fresh fruit, surrounded by bombed-out buildings.
Which, in a way, they were.

In April 1979, just six weeks after the ACR
session at Cargo, Martin Hannett was at Strawberry
Studios in Stockport with Joy Division to record *Unknown Pleasures*, which would be released in August
of that year. Strawberry housed a twenty-four-track
recording studio which owed its existence to the local
music scene of the 1960s.

In 1965, a modern open-air shopping cen-
tre was built in the shadow of the viaduct. Futuristic
and utopian, it was described in the *Stockport County*

---

[14] 16 February 1979.

Express in 1965 as 'space age'. The Merseyway shopping centre featured leading retailers including Woolworths, and Rumbelows, a clock tower lording it over the shoppers, rooftop car parks, and an open-air travelator – a motorised moving walkway – transporting shoppers between the ground and the upper floor.

Stockport in the mid-1960s was lively, with a handful of venues for touring and local beat groups, including the Essoldo, the Manor Lodge, and the Sinking Ship. Local acts included Four Just Men, and the Toggery Five who rehearsed at the Thatched House pub on Churchgate. They were formed in homage to a boutique called the Toggery.

The Toggery was owned by Mike Cohen, a celebrated clothes designer, who provided outfits for the likes of the Beatles. Cohen went on to become the first manager of the Hollies. Pete Maclaine, front man of Pete Maclaine & the Dakotas, had a job at the Toggery, as did Graham Nash, founder member of the Hollies.

Wayne Fontana & the Mindbenders were big on the local circuit and survived even after the departure of Wayne Fontana in 1965. Guitarist Eric Stewart took over lead vocals; their version of 'Groovy Kind of Love' was an international hit.

The Mockingbirds also emerged in the beat

group boom. Signing to Columbia, the Mockingbirds
intended their debut single would be 'For Your Love'
– written by the band's guitarist Graham Gouldman
during downtime at Bargains Unlimited in Salford,
the men's clothing shop where he worked – but the
record company disagreed. Meanwhile, the rejected
song was picked up by the Yardbirds whose version
of 'For Your Love' achieved Top Ten in both the UK
and the American charts. The Yardbirds had another
hit with a Gouldman composition, 'Heart Full of Soul',
then the Hollies hit the Top Five in the charts with
his 'Look Through Any Window', but Mockingbirds
singles continued to fail miserably.

By the end of 1968, both the Mindbenders
and the Mockingbirds had disbanded. Eric Stewart
moved on to a project of a different sort: Strawberry Studios. Founded by Peter Tattersall, Strawberry
began life as Inter-City Studios above the Nield and
Hardy record store. Eric Stewart very soon joined Tattersall in the venture, investing eight hundred pounds
in Inter-City to improve the facilities and the standard
of the equipment. At this point, the name was changed
to Strawberry Studios, in homage to the song 'Strawberry Fields Forever'.

The studios moved to Waterloo Road, and attracted extra financial support from Graham Gould-

man. In 1972, Eric Stewart, former Mockingbirds drummer Kevin Godley, Lol Creme, and Graham Gouldman – recording as 10cc – released a single, 'Donna', which kicked off great success for the band in the mid-1970s, boosted investment into the studio, and contributed to Strawberry's evolution into a high-profile and major recording facility. All four 10cc albums and their eight Top Ten singles were recorded at Strawberry, including the huge 1975 single 'I'm Not In Love'.

By the end of 1976, 10cc had split in half, with Godley and Creme leaving the band to pursue a separate career. Punk had announced its arrival – Tony Wilson presenting the debut TV performance of 'Anarchy in the UK' on his show on Granada. We were now just over ten years on from the ultra-modern Merseyway shopping centre, and the glorious success of local bands. It was a darker age. The numbers of large-scale industrial job losses were beginning to accelerate. At the Merseyway shopping centre, the outdoor travelator was often broken.

+

There was much to be said for the line-up of four in A Certain Ratio, but Tony Wilson was on the lookout for a drummer. He'd heard a young man in Wythenshawe, Donald Johnson, would be an asset, so he popped round one Friday evening after hosting the news on Granada, and Donald accepted the job. At the time, ACR rehearsed in the dirty and damp cellar of B.G Records on Little Underbank in Stockport.

In September 1979, soon after Donald had joined, Tony Wilson booked the group and Martin Hannett into Graveyard Studios to record a selection of songs the band were playing live. Although the recording was conceived as a demo, the success of the session convinced Wilson to make the songs available. With seven songs from the Graveyard recordings on one side, and a live recording from a show at the Electric Ballroom on the other, *The Graveyard and the Ballroom* was a cassette-only release, presented in a plastic sleeve in various colours; designed by Peter Saville, and all very lovely and collectible.

Across in the Big Apple, the artwork and other visuals for Grace Jones were invariably striking. Factory Records also knew these things mattered – by January 1980, the label, without any kind of budget, were establishing a reputation for pioneering, peculiar music beautifully packaged.

In November 1980, when Grace Jones met A Certain Ratio in Stockport, the plan they discussed was a collaboration on a cover version of a song by Talking Heads called 'Houses in Motion'. It was a more appropriate choice than Grace knew; in December 1979, A Certain Ratio had supported Talking Heads, leading lights in the New York scene.

For several years, many music lovers in Britain had been looking in wonderment at what was happening in New York. The Velvet Underground had set down a marker, and in their wake the New York Dolls, Patti Smith, and the scenes around CBGBs and Television were fascinating and ground-breaking. 'Those American bands were a different league,' Martin Moscrop recalls.

The tour was a great opportunity for A Certain Ratio, playing at venues like the Free Trade Hall in Manchester, Birmingham Odeon, and Newcastle City Hall. Martin recalls that Tina Weymouth taught Jez how to restring his bass, and the advantages of using a high-tech guitar tuner. 'We wouldn't be here now, doing what we do now, if we hadn't had that experience.'

Mid-1980, ACR delivered two of their finest works. First a stunning version of the deep funk song 'Shack Up', initially a hit for Banbarra in 1975, then they recorded 'Flight' for a single release on Factory; minimalist but also monumental, a triumph of a tune given huge depth and atmosphere by Martin Hannett.

That summer, the Factory family suffered a horrific blow when Joy Division singer Ian Curtis took his own life, with the band just days away from their first trip to the USA; the dates in the States were cancelled. Just a few months later, the surviving members, regrouped as New Order, were offered American dates for the new band in September 1980, solely around New York.

On this tour, New Order and ACR played venues including Tier 3, where, in amongst the audience, were the young men who went on to form the Beastie Boys. At Hurrah on 26 September, ACR met Martha 'Tilly' Tilson who went on to work with them. Ian Penman of the *New Musical Express* (*NME*), reviewing the show, was impressed with Hurrah, praising the architecture, layout, music policy (the music booker was Ruth Polsky, who went on to Danceteria). Reflecting on the trip to New York, Penman's review included this hope: 'I only wish we had a Hurrah or two over here.'[15]

ACR were in New York to play but also to record. Tony Wilson was eager for them to experience the city but also to further their profile. He had booked a studio for them, together with Hannett, with the aim of recording their first proper album.

---

[15] *NME*, 11 October 1980.

Eastern Arts Recording Studio was out in New Jersey.

ACR stayed in a loft on Hudson Street in Tribeca and travelled every day to New Jersey. 'New York was an amazing place in 1980,' says Martin Moscrop. 'We'd record in the day, into the evening and then get back on Manhattan and go out all night.'

The band visited jazz clubs including the Village Vanguard. One night out they saw a samba band; the rhythms, the energy and the power from a little stage packed with performers made a massive impact. Another time, they saw the Rock Steady Crew at the Roxy. A night Donald remembers: 'Simon kept trying to drag me over to watch a guy spinning on his head. I didn't believe him at first, I just thought he was drunk. But then I saw it and it was amazing'.[16]

Tony had been over to the States a couple of times before, remembers Martin. 'He was like an encyclopaedia of information. He'd take us to different places in New York and tell us all about that place.'

In March 1980, Studio 54 had closed, but even disco queen Grace Jones was already a little disillusioned by the scene.[17] In her memoirs, she suggests

---

[16] *Debris*, issue 13.
[17] Studio 54 reopened in September 1981, under new owners but, second time around, fell short of its legendary status.

that Studio 54 had become 'more about the hyped-up theatre and horseplay than about new music'.[18] In an echo of what had happened to punk, disco had become codified, almost stripped of all progressive elements. *Saturday Night Fever* was both a celebration of disco and its death knell. The disco scene had become commercialised. The excitement was elsewhere.

Martin recalls a Sunday afternoon they went to Central Park. 'One section of the park was taken up by Puerto Ricans playing congas and cowbells and jamming together. Another section was breakdancers, and another section was people roller-skating; hip hop had just started, so there was just so much to take in. As young men at the time it was inspirational.'

The loft apartment on Hudson Street, in amongst warehouse buildings, was basic; a parquet floor, whitewashed walls, and a bathroom. The band invested in six mattresses and six sheets. When they left, Chuck, the guy who owned the building, put all the mattresses and sheets into storage so if they returned they had bedding ready and waiting.

Michael Shamberg filmed A Certain Ratio in the Hudson Street loft playing percussion and inter-

---

[18] Jones, *Memoirs*, 151.

cut it with footage from the gigs (Tony had met Michael at a club on Union Square). Jez Kerr points out to me that the film *Tribeca* also features a glimpse of New Order manager Rob Gretton; I find him at 10:16 into the film, lying on his back in the corner having a smoke.[19]

Jez tells a story about Harvey Keitel being in the same block as the loft ACR were staying in. According to Jez, Robert De Niro rented a loft on the top floor; he was a friend of Chuck's. De Niro had lent his place to Harvey Keitel who was entertaining a girlfriend there at the same time ACR and Michael Shamberg were recording the video. The noise annoyed Mr Keitel who banged on the door, asking them how long they were going to be playing music for.

'Jez's story's slightly different to Pete's story, slightly different to the way I remember it,' says Martin. 'But you've got to go with one story really and I think Jez's story is the best one [both laugh].'

So what's your story? Just so that I can hear it.

'My story is that we were in the loft and I don't know if it was Harvey Keitel's wife or Robert De Niro's: I thought it was Robert De Niro's wife. I thought it was Robert De Niro staying in the loft above us. And we

---

[19] https://youtu.be/VlUGid-PLBY5

were playing football in the loft and she came banging
on the door and said, "Can you guys stop playing bas-
ketball in the loft?" And we said [putting on an extra
strong Northern accent], "We're not playing basket-
ball, we're playing football."'

We both laugh. 'That's how I remember it
anyway,' says Martin.

There's no debate over how ESG made their
way into the Factory Records catalogue. ESG were
an art-funk band from the Bronx, who supported A
Certain Ratio at one of their shows in New York and
impressed the band, and Tony Wilson too. Having finished the album early, ACR had three days left in the
studio, so gave the studio time to ESG. Martin Hannett produced the sessions at Eastern Arts and then
he took the tapes back to Strawberry for the final mix.
The songs 'Moody', 'You're No Good', and 'UFO' were
all later released by Factory Records.

Tony Wilson was always championing Manchester, but New York mesmerised him, as it did Rob
Gretton. Ian Penman was spot-on about Hurrah. The
experiences of Factory, ACR and New Order in the Big
Apple bore fruit in 1982 when the Haçienda opened,
Tony later explaining that the club had been inspired
by visits to Hurrah and Danceteria. 'They were cool
clubs. And if New York had them, then why the fuck

didn't Manchester?'[20] In May 1982, ESG flew from New York to play the opening night at the Haçienda. The club wouldn't have happened if Tony Wilson, Rob Gretton and New Order hadn't been as intoxicated and inspired by New York as they were.

+

After three disco albums recorded with Tom Moulton, Grace Jones wanted a new direction, born of a desire to evolve as an artist, and a belief, in her words, that 'disco was becoming a corporate monster'.[21] Her management had plans for her, a showbiz career mapped out: start with disco and then go to Vegas. But she was unhappy. Grace recalls: 'I had a battle with them because I thought more radically and they were safe, to the point of cosy.'

      To ease the tension and give Grace a chance to reset her career, her management stepped down and arranged for her to sign direct to Island Records. Island had been distributing the music released by Beam Junction but the Island boss didn't even know

---

[20] Quoted in James Nice, *Shadowplayers: The Rise and Fall of Factory Records* (Aurum Press Ltd, 2010), 133.
[21] Jones, *Memoirs*, 168.

this until he researched her work after being alert-ed to her talents by journalist Nik Cohn. The Island boss was Chris Blackwell. His passions included reg-gae and folk, but not disco: 'Grace's disco world was hugely different for Island and very different for me,' he writes in his autobiography *The Islander: My Life in Music and Beyond*.[22]

Blackwell appreciated some of the back cata-logue, including 'La Vie en rose', but her second and third albums he thought were disappointingly bland and not at all reflective of her off-centre risk-taking per-sonality, describing them as 'More drum machine than Grace, which is an outrage really, as Grace was no face-less singer but a vocal artist and a living work of art.'[23]

Grace had begun working with photographer and graphic designer Jean-Paul Goude a couple of years earlier, and they had become a couple; early in 1979 she became pregnant, the child due a few weeks before Christmas. In Grace's words, Goude, a former art director at *Esquire* magazine in New York, 'trans-formed the story of my life into a series of visions and fantasies.'[24]

---

[22] Chris Blackwell, *The Islander: My Life in Music and Beyond* (Nine Eight Books, 2022), 299.
[23] Ibid., 300.
[24] Jones, *Memoirs*, 204.

The first photo session with Goude resulted in a stunning image: Grace Jones naked and shining, with one foot in the air. Bold, balletic, erotic. Blackwell and Grace resolved to make music that matched the Jean-Paul Goude photographs. In her memoirs she talks of the 'flimsy disco sheen being ripped back'.[25]

After the film *Saturday Night Fever*, disco needed time to return to its underground roots, to find its soul again. Rather than at Studio 54, raw thrills were to be found at no-frills venues with great sound systems, and DJs playing an eclectic mix.

In her descriptions of the shake-up of clubbing in the first years of the 1980s, Grace also mentions several music venues including some that hosted the short New Order and ACR tour. Clubs like Danceteria she declared 'creative places'. At Tier 3, the artist Jean-Michel Basquiat would occasionally DJ (his involvement at Tier 3 also included painting a mural on the wall between the bar room and the music room). The gulf that existed in 1978 between ACR at Band on the Wall and Grace Jones at Studio 54 was closing.

Grace felt at home around visual artists. A few years into the 1980s, she particularly bonded with Keith Haring. Their collaborations included Haring

---

[25] Ibid., 298.

painting a skirt for her to wear in her 'I'm Not Perfect (But I'm Perfect for You)' video (directed by Andy
Warhol).

The album showcasing the new direction
would be recorded in Nassau, in the Bahamas; at Compass Point Studios built by Chris Blackwell. Blackwell
gathered a great team of musicians for the project –
dubbed the Compass Point All Stars – including Sly
and Robbie, and Wally Badarou. Grace Jones had re-
newed enthusiasm and a clear aim, thanks to Blackwell. 'He didn't care that I sounded like a man or an
entity; he simply wanted my voice to be strong.'[26]

+

Nick Stewart started work as an A&R at Island Records
in the summer of 1979. Soon after taking the job, he
was phoned by Chris Blackwell and informed of the
plans for the new Grace Jones album and that they'd
decided to start with the song 'Warm Leatherette'.
'Warm Leatherette' was a single by the Normal released
in May 1978 (a double A-side, partnered by 'TVOD').
The Normal was a solo project by Daniel Miller, an
admirer of the likes of Can and Cabaret Voltaire. Plug-

---

[26] Blackwell, *The Islander*, 213.

ging into the DIY spirit of the time, he created a record label to release the single; and called it Mute.

Blackwell told his new A&R man that he needed more ideas. Nick suggested 'Love is the Drug' by Roxy Music, and 'She's Lost Control' by Joy Division (from Joy Division's debut album, which had been released the same month as he arrived at Island). Nick also suggested 'Private Life', a track written by Chrissie Hynde on the debut album by the Pretenders.

'Private Life' was released as a single on 27 June 1980. The B-side was 'She's Lost Control' which hadn't been included on final track listing for the *Warm Leatherette* album despite being part of the same Compass Point sessions. Recorded several months before Ian Curtis died, it was the first Joy Division cover version released, and still ranks among the very best.

In being drawn to the harsher aesthetic of the likes of the Normal, and the Factory acts, Grace Jones was rejecting airbrushing in favour of something fiercer, more disruptive. She had no idea who Joy Division were, however. 'I just loved the song, I let the words take me over. I heard "lost control" and that was enough for me. I decided, OK, that's not written for me, but I think it might have been written about me.'[27]

---

[27] Jones, *Memoirs*, 223.

Nick was a big fan of Factory Records. 'Everything that Factory did I thought was really cool,' he says. During discussions about Grace Jones covering 'She's Lost Control', he made an attempt to sign Joy Division ('Rob Gretton just laughed'), but captured another Factory act, the Distractions. 'I thought they were like the Byrds reincarnated.'

Nick's next signing to Island was an Irish band called U2. U2 loved *Unknown Pleasures*, so Martin Hannett was asked to produce Island's first U2 single, '11 O'Clock Tick Tock'. U2 met Hannett at Strawberry Studios to discuss the idea, although it was decided to record in Dublin, at Windmill Lane Studios. Hannett went over there, and took a lot of acid. The single was released in May 1980, but failed to chart, and was also left off the first U2 album, *Boy*.

'Private Life' fared better. It became the first hit for Grace Jones in the UK. A promotional trip to Britain in August 1980 included an appearance on *Top of the Pops* and an interview with *The Face*. Mid-November, Grace returned, with a packed schedule over several days. Talk of collaborating with A Certain Ratio had progressed. In the Ian Penman interview in *NME*, Grace says it was her decision to cover 'Houses in Motion'. Penman points out that the opening line might well have amused her, with its inadvertent namecheck: 'For a long time I felt without style or grace'.

I ask Nick to confirm whose idea it was for the collaboration. 'I knew you would ask me this,' he says. 'And I'm really sorry, I just don't know. I know there's a tape, or there's something somewhere. But I have no idea. I suppose because of what had happened with "She's Lost Control", they thought they might be able to do something.'

I wait, hoping he might suddenly retrieve the details. 'I am weak on this, sorry. I remember going,' says Nick. 'And I do remember taking her in, I remember meeting the band. I've never done a drug in my life so I can't blame that, but my memory is hazy, Dave.'

I tell Donald from ACR that I love the thought of worlds colliding. Jet-setting Grace Jones who'd headlined New Year's Eve at Studio 54 in the presence of Andy Warhol, Michael Jackson, the glitterati. No expense spared on the outfit. Then three albums later she's walking along Waterloo Road in Stockport to meet A Certain Ratio, lads living in Hulme, and Wythenshawe, signed to a small label operating from a front bedroom of a house in Withington. He laughs. 'Absolutely, yeah. That was probably the most surreal thing for me as well, that I was there and knowing that all that happened.'

The Stockport visit was arranged for the day after she was in Manchester for a live interview at the

BBC studios on a chat show hosted by Russell Harty on Tuesday 18 November 1980. The show's other guest was royal photographer and the Queen's cousin, Patrick Lichfield. This turned into one of the most memorable moments in the history of television. I read Nick a quote from Grace: 'I slapped Russell Harty as I'd done some bad cocaine earlier and was feeling exhausted and had no idea where I was. It seemed I was hallucinating that I was on a live chat show and the host was ignoring me.'[28]

'Well, that's perfectly fair,' Nick replies.

Grace's intention was to turn up, make conversation, perform 'Love is the Drug', and then get to the hotel booked for her in Liverpool. Russell Harty didn't seem particularly interested in her story, and, partly owing to the strange alignment of the chairs on set, spent some time with his back to her. Grace says Harty was 'damp with excitement' at the presence of Lord Lichfield. Once he'd finished talking to Grace, he turned away completely to chat to Lord Lichfield. 'Don't turn your back on me anymore,' she says, poking him in the back. Things escalate, she begins aiming slaps at him, hitting him; more to 'humiliate him than to hurt,' she later explained. It was wild television. In the tabloid

---

[28] Ibid., 237.

newspapers it was a sensation. Grace Jones was unre-pentant: 'He never got so much press in his life.'

That evening Grace stayed at the Atlantic Towers Hotel on Chapel Street, which was a swish place to stay on the Liverpool waterfront (the hotel is now part of the Mercure chain); opened in 1972, designed to look like the bow of a ship, and the haunt of celebrity guests like Elton John, and Shirley Bassey.

The following day, before Grace was due at Strawberry, her itinerary kept her in Liverpool for a day of filming a Granada TV show called *Celebration*. At that time, Granada, as well as occupying a good few acres at their original home on the edge of Manchester city centre, also had a studio on Albert Dock in Liverpool. The docks were once a symbol of Liverpool's mercantile power, but having fallen into disrepair, they were now a symbol of economic disaster.

Grace shared her thoughts about Liverpool with Ian Penman in *NME* a week or two later; she said it felt very empty of people but the waterside industrial remains were intriguing: 'These huge columns, and all the windows are busted glass. Very ghostly looking... with a hint of the end of the world about it.' This was part of the bleak environment out of which bands including Teardrop Explodes, Wah Heat, Pink Military, and Echo & the Bunnymen were then emerging.

Grace was three hours late at the filming, mostly because her timekeeping was habitually problematic. At some point, an official press shot was taken to feed the media's interest. The photograph featured Grace aiming a punch at boxer John Conteh in a playful reference to the blows she rained down on Mr Harty, while George Melly looks on (it's not clear exactly how these two men came to be her supporting cast).

The only reference I can find to Grace Jones acknowledging or describing her encounter with A Certain Ratio at Strawberry is in *NME*, in the same interview as she discussed her Liverpool visit. She says A Certain Ratio were 'real cute', and she found them 'very interesting, I like the way they dress'. It was usual for Jean-Paul Goude to oversee her haircuts, but after meeting ACR, Grace had a hint of hair envy. 'I wonder who cuts their hair? I should go to their barbers.'

In the days prior to meeting Grace Jones, A Certain Ratio prepared two versions of 'Houses in Motion', one self-produced with guide vocals by Jez, and the other an instrumental version by Martin Hannett more or less ready for Grace to add her vocals to. They'd also decided the ACR tune 'And Then Again' (the B-side of 'Flight') could work with Grace's vocals so they recorded an instrumental version of that too.

Factory had rented Strawberry for several

consecutive all-night sessions to work on the tracks, and for the Grace Jones visit. The band had begun to congregate around 9 p.m., joined by Tony Wilson and the photographer Kevin Cummins who Tony had alerted and invited to document the occasion.

Eventually Grace arrived, with Nick Stewart and also Tony Michaelides, her radio and TV plugger from Island Records (who'd been with her all day). It's thought that Tony Wilson had left by the time she arrived; there aren't photos of him at Strawberry that evening. Kevin remembers a lot of hanging around, no one doing much except smoking weed.

The pubs shut at ten thirty; this was 1980, in Stockport. One thing ACR remember is that, on arrival, Grace asked for some wine. It was virtually impossible to get wine at eleven o'clock at night in Stockport. However, two bottles of wine were purchased from a local Indian restaurant just closing up.

Kevin's photos were taken in the entrance foyer at Strawberry. One features Martin Hannett with Grace, and Simon Topping looking dubious in the background. Don doesn't appear on any of the photographs although he can recall meeting Grace Jones, but doubts he had any kind of earth-shattering conversation with her.

The visit was never intended to include Grace

recording vocals for either of the songs, but neverthe-less, she was at the studios for several hours, and had a listen to the prepared tracks, even though they were still being tweaked by Martin Hannett. The atmo-sphere was positive, says Martin Moscrop. 'She was really into the idea, she liked the backing track, she got on with Martin [Hannett].'

In a subsequent news piece in *NME*, a Cum-mins photo of Simon Topping with Grace is accompa-nied by a hundred and fifty words or so.[29] Pete Terrell says: 'The song was her choice, not ours, but the idea of working together is OK.' A wary, if not weary, Si-mon Topping tells the journalist he really doesn't want to say anything, but that was often the way.

Behind the scenes, Tony Wilson was keen to take the collaboration as far as he could, Martin Mo-scrop told me recently. 'He put it to us that we should consider going to Barbados to record a whole album with Martin Hannett for Grace Jones. Nick will tell you about this.'

Nick isn't really sure, I tell Martin. And also he can't work out why the project was shelved.

'Well, I think when Chris Blackwell found out about the idea, he wasn't very happy.'

---

[29] *NME*, 29 November 1980.

I share with Don my assessment that nothing progressed with the idea after the encounter at Stockport partly because of the loyalty of Chris Blackwell and Grace Jones to the Compass Point All Stars but possibly also because of the timing. The *Warm Leatherette* album had come out and 'Private Life' had been a big hit. Blackwell had forward plans; in fact, recording of the *Nightclubbing* album at Compass Point was well advanced. However interesting the idea of working with ACR was, where would that have fitted in her schedule?

Don: 'I think it was always a great idea, but nobody sat down and worked out the practicalities of it. Unless you keep talking about it, you don't really remember. And Ratio are pretty much like that all the time. We just keep moving. Trying to do stuff that's not obvious.'

+

In the weeks after they met, both Grace Jones and A Certain Ratio turned their attentions to new albums. *Nightclubbing* saw the light of day in May 1981. It had more input from Grace than *Warm Leatherette* did, including several contributions to the songwriting, as she explained to *Sounds*: 'You have to have the time. I just had a baby and I was touring at the same time – so many things were happening. But I've been working on things with the new one.'[30]

The *Nightclubbing* album is blessed with superb tracks, including 'Pull Up to the Bumper', 'Walking in the Rain', and 'Libertango', a vignette about Paris nightlife. The Goude sleeve is forceful and fabulous; a head-and-padded-shoulders view of Grace with a severe flat-top haircut and a cigarette on her lips, staring straight at the viewer, impregnable.

In 1981 ACR recorded a new album, *Sextet*, this time without Martin Hannett. The record features vocals by Martha 'Tilly' Tilson, with Simon Topping concentrating on trumpet and percussion (he'd always admitted to being a reluctant frontman). The influence of the New York trip was strong; a looser Latin sound was all over *Sextet* (most notably on 'Skipscada'), all wonderfully fused with ACR's moody post-punk edge.

ACR and Factory's connections with the Big Apple strengthened in the following years. The passionate championing of Factory acts by Michael Shamberg and Ruth Polsky contributed to this. In 1983, New Order recorded 'Confusion' in Manhattan under the direction of producer Arthur Baker, who

---

[30] *Sounds*, 23 August 1980.

also appears in the video filmed at a club called the Funhouse. The band are seen arriving and hanging out in the DJ box with the DJ, John 'Jellybean' Benitez.

ACR had met Grace Jones at a time when her star was in its ascendancy, but had an encounter with another female music icon two years later, one who was then unknown. In 1982, A Certain Ratio played the Danceteria; the support act was Madonna; her first-ever live performance. Madonna was one of the club's regulars – and the girlfriend of resident DJ Mark Kamins. She badgered Ruth Polsky for the support slot. To help draw a crowd to see ACR and Madonna, Ruth Polsky printed special invitations and promised a free buffet. I've always been intrigued about what was included in the buffet, but no one can recall seeing sandwiches. Drugs yes, sandwiches no.

Chuck Low, De Niro's landlord in Tribeca, again provided sleeping space for A Certain Ratio on their 1982 visit. Chuck's life was about to take an exciting turn when De Niro helped secure him some film work. In *Goodfellas*, he's knifed to death in the back of the head by Joe Pesci.

Daniel Miller – inspiration for Grace Jones's evolution as an artist with his 'Warm Leatherette' single – took what he'd learned from releasing the record on his own Mute label and began putting out music by the likes of Fad Gadget and DAF. Then a band called Depeche Mode joined Mute; fifteen studio albums later, they're still sharing massive success. And if the connections aren't dizzying enough, in 2018 Daniel Miller and Mute began reissuing A Certain Ratio's back catalogue, which led to ACR releasing albums of new material, including *ACR Loco* (2020), a related album *Loco Remezclada* (2020), and *1982* (2023). ACR's thirteenth studio album, *It All Comes Down To This*, released in 2024 and produced by Dan Carey, melds funked-up ACR with heavy, biting, off-kilter sounds. Every time I've talked with any of the band about meeting Grace Jones, they also enthuse about the new album, with good reason.

A box set of ACR material released by Mute includes their versions of 'Houses in Motion', using the original 1980 tapes. It's very close to the original but a few things sounded a little out of time, so a bit of work was needed to get that right. The only things actually added were a new clap and some trumpet.

Strawberry Studios has been closed for over thirty years. In 2017, the studios featured in an exhibition at Stockport Museum. Strawberry has symbolic significance. The Beatles left Liverpool and set up their base and their record label in London. Strawberry in Stockport, however, lent strength to the instincts of people like Tony Wilson; he saw Factory Records as a vehiclc to resist the dominance of London and instead build a creative music scene locally. To do for music what Granada were doing in television.

Wilson's interest in the local music scene, though, extended only as far as it impacted on his overriding interest – the world of ideas. Factory Records was based in Manchester but the label nurtured connections well beyond the city. Within a year or two of forming, they'd built links to Belgium, appointed Mark Reeder their representative in Berlin, and in New York gave a guiding role to Michael Shamberg (he went on to become central to Factory's operations in the States).

Manchester celebrates itself relentlessly, sometimes with a tendency to be blind to the value of activity elsewhere. This wasn't Wilson's way. Tony would also have known some of the missing parts to this story. If he didn't have the facts, he'd have explained the vision. He'd have given us some answers. He'd also have had a good guess whether Marianne Faithfull has ever been to Studio 54, where the sandwiches were at Danceteria, and who exactly was annoyed by the noise from ACR's Hudson Street loft. In the meantime, let's allow a bit of mystery into this history.

+

This is how it begins. A creative journey starting somewhere unexpected, with something far from fully formed. It begins at Bargains Unlimited, down near Salford Docks, Graham Gouldman hiding away to write songs that turned into hits that helped Peter Tattersall to finance the evolution of Strawberry Studios. Creativity begins at the Toggery on Mersey Square, opposite Boots; Graham Nash working there, and less than a decade later being part of Crosby, Stills, Nash & Young.

Grace Jones tells us that disco started 'in private gay clubs with great music and the best, most fanatical DJs.'[31] Factory formed to put on gigs away from the centre of the city, once a week, in a former social club for bus drivers. A Certain Ratio bed down on mattresses in a loft in Tribeca. Sonic Youth tour Europe saving cash by sleeping on floors.

Creative characters with self-belief, some luck, and a good look are present in every generation, but in Britain at the end of the 1970s into the 1980s particular energies in the era propelled underground culture. These included the DIY attitudes of punk, and,

---

[31] *The Face*, October 1980.

in addition – in amongst the very real social disintegration and the widespread personal traumas deindustrialisation had brought about – the broken economy gave young people, especially those who were able to game the benefits system, room to dream. And rooms in which to dream; sites where like-minded folk gathered. Boutiques, record shops, basement venues attracted the music lovers, and mavericks, the confident and stylish but also the self-conscious and abashed, and the talents who've been told their face doesn't fit.

The unlikely sight of Grace Jones in the murky streets of post-industrial Stockport certainly lends itself to incredulity and questions. But one of the questions could be: why not Stockport?

It might not quite have been a case of Grace Jones being in the right place at the right time, as she was when she was on the stage at Studio 54 on New Year's Eve. But the idea is not as far-fetched as it would appear. Stockport is the kind of place that lacks sparkle or high profile and is too easily written off. When Engels called it 'repellent' he was viewing it from the railway viaduct. Down amongst the people he may have had his preconceptions confounded, met individuals with love in their hearts, and/or extraordinary abilities, and perhaps groups of people with collective ambition.

Stockport still wasn't particularly easy on the eye, but around the time Grace Jones was there, many similar towns lost in physical and economic decline – and a long way from the centre of political power – were making a magnificent contribution to music culture. Throbbing Gristle in Hull, for example, and reggae soundsystems and the Pop Group in Bristol. In Coventry, Jerry Dammers had pulled Two-Tone together, releasing music by the Specials, Madness, the Selecter and the Beat.

In that era, in unlovable function rooms in old pubs and grubby basement venues, new episodes in music history were being created. Not least when the Human League performed at the Limit in Sheffield on a Monday night in September 1978 (free admission). Or the Cure supported by Teardrop Explodes appeared at the F Club in Leeds in March 1979 (tickets £1.50).

1980 Stockport wasn't thriving – the big employers were long since bankrupt – but dozens of creative journeys were about to begin, in spaces that promised a taste of the good life – that, in some cases, and in retrospect – had an impact on the wider music world.

Paul Morley worked at a secondhand bookshop on Hillgate in 1975/6, at home among novels by JG Ballard, radical newspapers like *Mole Express*, and works by William Burroughs; taking from them knowledge, and weird alternative ways of thinking, which helped propel him towards a career in journalism. The shop also attracted young customers like Magazine's bass player Barry Adamson, and Martin Fry, several years before he fronted ABC.

In 1980, there weren't many places for young bands, New Wave or otherwise, to play – the many pubs featuring live music were dominated by an older generation. A band called Belgian Bitch – who were inspired by Bowie, Be Bop Deluxe and punk – improvised, gained access to a rooftop in the Merseyway shopping centre and played a free, impromptu gig one Saturday afternoon. Their music was released by Phil Ellis who ran Out of Town Records, based at Hologram Studios in the Market Place in Stockport opposite the Boar's Head (a less sophisticated but cheaper studio than Strawberry, it was where, in 1982, Mick Hucknall's band the Frantic Elevators recorded 'Holding Back the Years', way before the version by Simply Red).

Jason Boardman, veteran DJ and co-founder of the club night Aficionado, was fourteen years old in 1980. He bought 'Private Life' from B.G Records on Little Underbank. There were several places youngsters interested in music and alternative activity would congregate. 'B.G was the epicentre,' Jason says. 'You could get records very easily, at Woolworths, Boots – almost everywhere had a record counter – but B.G was the cutting-edge, and it would be mobbed. It was like a badge of honour walking round with a bag from B.G.' In addition, he reckons at least two of the tracks on his acclaimed 2023 sixteen-track compilation record released to mark twenty-five years of Aficionado were records he'd first sourced in the 1980s at another shop in the town, the 78 Record Exchange on Lower Hillgate.

Jason had no sense that Stockport lacked anything. It felt lively, exciting; it was what he calls his 'playground'. He frequented clothes shops including Crazy Face on Tiviot Dale (close to where the cinema complex, the Light, is now situated). Aged fourteen, he was working there most Saturdays. Crazy Face co-owner Joe Moss opened premises in Manchester city centre; and became the first manager of the Smiths. In February 1983, he funded the recording of the first Smiths single, 'Hand in Glove'. Joe booked a one-day recording session at Strawberry Studios, at a cost of £250.

Next door to the Crazy Face shop at Tiviot Dale there was a hairdressing salon called Gareth & Colin Hairdressers co-owned by Gareth Evans who later managed the Stone Roses. Gareth took over as Roses manager from Howard Jones, a former manager of the Haçienda. Howard had organised the first Roses single, also recorded at Strawberry (where else?), and with Martin Hannett (who else?).

A five-minute walk from Strawberry Studios, side by side; two future managers of two of the foremost bands of the 1980s were at work. As Joe's son, David Moss, says, 'Tiviot Dale is the meeting point of the rivers Goyt and Tame, where the Mersey forms, and is clearly a magical location'.[32] And almost seventy miles from where the Mersey flows past Albert Dock and into the sea.

In 1980, activity in Stockport took place at a time of austerity and economic depression. In the current era, what's different? There's a new, exhausting, period of austerity and economic depression, but this time perhaps there's one change that gives Stockport an advantage; neighbouring Manchester has enjoyed – if that's the word – economic regeneration, providing jobs and retails excitements, but burying some of the opportunities for unconventional, undercapitalised activity. Stockport offers a cheaper, less gentrified experience.

------

[32] https://digimoss.co.uk/2023/12/12/the-crazy-face-factory/

Notable in the present century: the release of Mr Scruff's mad samba single 'Stockport Carnival' (Scruff has always talked up his Stockport home, including the fabulousness of the railway viaduct); John Barratt of Seven Miles Out Records runs tours of Stockport concentrating on significant sites of the town's music history; in 2014, Moovin Festival was founded by Herbie Saccani who ran the dance music department of Double Four Records, when the shop was situated on Stockport's historic Lower Hillgate.

Recently, feeding into the burgeoning activity in Stockport, the Council embarked on a regeneration programme, covering the areas around Little Underbank, Mealhouse Brow and Lower Hillgate. There's now a sizeable and growing community of independent and creative enterprises round there and the old Market Square, including café bars, bookshops, restaurants (including the acclaimed Where The Light Gets In). Stockport has been christened the New Berlin by DJ Luke Unabomber and declared 2023 Greater Manchester Town of Culture.

SK1 record shop and café on Little Underbank, established in 2018 on the opposite side of the road to where B.G Records had been situated, holds monthly street parties – you'll find Jason Boardman on the decks, alongside guest DJs of all sorts. These parties have attracted huge interest, a great reputation, and, most significantly, support from the local council.

Local band Blossoms talk up Stockport at every opportunity; their packed show at Stockport County's football stadium in June 2019 energised the town in a remarkable way. Three of their four albums have reached number 1 on the UK album charts (their debut being the exception). Frontman Tom Ogden and his wife Katie have invested in several local ventures, including opening their own speakeasy cocktail bar, Bohemian Arts Club.

In my conversations with Don, we discuss the importance of self-belief, allies, cheap space, a collective energy in the air. He also talks of 'having a working attitude about making things happen regardless of what you've got'.

Things, but big things. The nature of Tony Wilson's ambition was like, 'Oh, we can change the world.'

'Absolutely,' says Don.

Don and I discuss this more, and I suggest that in a lot of the activity that was going on, people were obviously ambitious to do good things – the bands, of course, and Michael Shamberg, Ruth Polsky, Martin Hannett, the Factory people – but nobody seems to have been motivated solely by the idea of fame and riches.

Don: 'I didn't even know what we got paid back in those days doing whatever. Obviously, people can't run and do things forever for nothing; that evolves as well. But there was a lot of that "let's just do it". But, yes, you just wanted to be around and do something.'

The meaning of 'Houses in Motion' is opaque but its power to connect is direct. It seems as if the alienated narrator, aware that dreams might reach a dead end, is walking a line through life, trying to keep things together, exhibiting just enough faith to continue.

This is how it begins:[33]

For a long time I felt without style or grace
Wearing shoes with no socks in cold weather
I knew my heart was in the right place
I knew I'd be able to do these things

---

[33] 'Houses in Motion' lyrics © Downtown Music Publishing, Universal Music Publishing Group, Warner Chappell Music, Inc.

ORIGINAL ILLUSTRATION & COVER DESIGN
Zoë McLean, Manchester
zoe@confingopublishing.uk

TYPESETTING
John Oakey, Penrith
johnoakey1@gmail.com

BODY TYPE
*Minion 3, an updated and expanded version of
Robert Slimbach's early 90s design for Adobe.*

COVER TYPE
*Futura PT, developed at ParaType in 1995 by Vladimir
Yefimov, expands on the classic geometric sans-serif
typeface Futura designed by Paul Renner in 1927.*

Searching For Love:
Courtney Love in Liverpool, 1982

'Meticulously researched, Haslam unpicks and unravels the barrage of myths told about Love in Liverpool'
Anokhi Shah

'I loved every second of this read! A book littered with truth and adventure at every turn'
Emma Aylett

My Second Home: Sylvia Plath in Paris, 1956

'Delicately balanced between light and dark and inspiringly researched'
Shaun Tomkiss

'It is absolutely beautiful, the last few pages nearly brought me to tears. It is such a moving and unique account'
Rosie Day

All You Need is Dynamite: Acid, the Angry Brigade, and the End of the Sixties

'A highly enthralling, enchanting story... it's dynamite'
Ryan Walker

'An important piece of work - it was a pleasure to spend time with it'
John McCready

Not All Roses: The Life & Times of Stephen Cresser

'A brilliant short read and a moving, and evocative, piece of writing'
John Harris

'Really beautiful. Honest brutal gentle and very moving
but there's hope too'
Luke Unabomber

Adventure Everywhere: Pablo Picasso's Paris Nightlife

'Smutty, seedy & incredibly detailed'
RGM Magazine

'Brilliant. I read it in one sitting'
Jason Williamson (Sleaford Mods)